The Years Between by Rudyard Kipling

Rudyard Kipling: A great Victorian, a great writer of Empire, a great man.

Rudyard Kipling was one of the most popular writers of prose and poetry in the late 19th and 20th Century and awarded the Noble Prize for Literature in 1907.

Born in Bombay on 30th December 1865, as was the custom in those days, he and his sister were sent back to England when he was 5. The ill-treatment and cruelty by the couple who they boarded with in Portsmouth, Kipling himself suggested, contributed to the onset of his literary life. This was further enhanced by his return to India at age 16 to work on a local paper, as not only did this result in him writing constantly but also made him explore issues of identity and national allegiance which pervade much of his work.

Whilst he is best remembered for his classic children's stories and his popular poem 'If…' he is also regarded as a major innovator in the art of the short story.

Index of Contents

I0158401

The Benefactors

Ah! What avails the classic bent
   And what the cultured word,
Against the undoctored incident
   That actually occurred?

And what is Art whereto we press
   Through paint and prose and rhyme—
When Nature in her nakedness
   Defeats us every time?

It is not learning, grace nor gear,
   Nor easy meat and drink,
But bitter pinch of pain and fear
   That makes creation think

When in this world's unpleasing youth
   Our god-like race began,
The longest arm, the sharpest tooth,
   Gave man control of man;

Till, bruised and bitten to the bone

And taught by pain and fear,
He learned to deal the far-off stone,
  And poke the long, safe spear.

So tooth and nail were obsolete
  As means against a foe,
Till, bored by uniform defeat,
  Some genius built the bow.

Then stone and javelin proved as vain
  As old-time tooth and nail;
Till, spurred anew by fear and pain,
  Man fashioned coats of mail.

Then was there safety for the rich
  And danger for the poor,
Till someone mixed a powder which
  Redressed the scale once more.

Helmet and armour disappeared
  With sword and bow and pike,
And, when the smoke of battle cleared,
  All men were armed alike. . . .

And when ten million such were slain
  To please one crazy king,
Man, schooled in bulk by fear and pain,
  Grew weary of the thing;

And, at the very hour designed,
  To enslave him past recall,
His tooth-stone-arrow-gun-shy mind
  Turned and abolished all.

All Power, each Tyrant, every Mob
  Whose head has grown too large,
Ends by destroying its own job
  And works its own discharge;

And Man, whose mere necessities
  Move all things from his path,
Trembles meanwhile at their decrees,
  And deprecates their wrath!

To the Judge of Right and Wrong
　　With Whom fulfilment lies
Our purpose and our power belong,
　　Our faith and sacrifice,

Let Freedom's Land rejoice!
　　Our ancient bonds are riven;
Once more to us the eternal choice
　　Of Good or Ill is given.

Not at a little cost,
　　Hardly by prayer or tears,
Shall we recover the road we lost
　　In the drugged and doubting years.

But, after the fires and the wrath,
　　But, after searching and pain,
His Mercy opens us a path
　　To live with ourselves again.

In the Gates of Death rejoice!
　　We see and hold the good—
Bear witness, Earth, we have made our choice
　　With Freedom's brotherhood!

Then praise the Lord Most High
　　Whose Strength hath saved us whole,
Who bade us choose that the Flesh should die
　　And not the living Soul!

To the God in Man displayed—
　　Wheree'er we see that Birth,
Be love and understanding paid
　　As never yet on earth!

To the Spirit that moves in Man,
　　On Whom all worlds depend,
Be Glory since our world began
　　And service to the end!

"The City of Brass"

Here was a people whom after their works thou shalt see wept over for their lost dominion: and in this palace is the last information respecting lords collected in the dust.

In a land that the sand overlays—the ways to her gates are untrod—
A multitude ended their days whose fates were made splendid by God,
Till they grew drunk and were smitten with madness and went to their fall,
And of these is a story written: but Allah Alone knoweth all!

When the wine stirred in their heart their bosoms dilated,
They rose to suppose themselves kings over all things created—
To decree a new earth at a birth without labour or sorrow—
To declare: "We prepare it to-day and inherit to-morrow."

They chose themselves prophets and priests of minute understanding,
Men swift to see done, and outrun, their extremest commanding—
Of the tribe which describe with a jibe the perversions of Justice—
Panders avowed to the crowd whatsoever its lust is.

Swiftly these pulled down the walls that their fathers had made them—
The impregnable ramparts of old, they razed and relaid them
As playgrounds of pleasure and leisure with limitless entries,
And havens of rest for the wastrels where once walked the sentries;
And because there was need of more pay for the shouters and marchers,
They disbanded in face of their foemen their yeomen and archers.

They replied to their well-wishers' fears—to their enemies' laughter,
Saying: "Peace! We have fashioned a God Which shall save us hereafter.
We ascribe all dominion to man in his factions conferring,
And have given to numbers the Name of the Wisdom unerring."

They said: "Who has hate in his soul? Who has envied his neighbour?
Let him arise and control both that man and his labour."
They said: "Who is eaten by sloth? Whose unthrift has destroyed him?
He shall levy a tribute from all because none have employed him."
They said: "Who hath toiled, who hath striven, and gathered possession?
Let him be spoiled. He hath given full proof of transgression."

They said: "Who is irked by the Law? Though we may not remove it,
If he lend us his aid in this raid, we will set him above it!"
So the robber did judgment again upon such as displeased him,
The slayer, too, boasted his slain, and the judges released him.

As for their kinsmen far off, on the skirts of the nation,
They harried all earth to make sure none escaped reprobation,
They awakened unrest for a jest in their newly-won borders,
And jeered at the blood of their brethren betrayed by their orders.

They instructed the ruled to rebel, their rulers to aid them;
And, since such as obeyed them not fell, their Viceroys obeyed them.

When the riotous set them at naught they said: "Praise the upheaval!
For the show and the word and the thought of Dominion is evil!"

They unwound and flung from them with rage, as a rag that defiled them
The imperial gains of the age which their forefathers piled them.
They ran panting in haste to lay waste and embitter for ever
The wellsprings of Wisdom and Strength which are Faith and Endeavour.

They nosed out and digged up and dragged forth and exposed to derision
All doctrine of purpose and worth and restraint and prevision:
And it ceased, and God granted them all things for which they had striven,
And the heart of a beast in the place of a man's heart was given. . .

When they were fullest of wine and most flagrant in error,
Out of the sea rose a sign—out of Heaven a terror.
Then they saw, then they heard, then they knew—for none troubled to hide it,
An host had prepared their destruction, but still they denied it.

They denied what they dared not abide if it came to the trial,
But the Sword that was forged while they lied did not heed their denial.
It drove home, and no time was allowed to the crowd that was driven.

The preposterous-minded were cowed—they thought time would be given.
There was no need of a steed nor a lance to pursue them;
It was decreed their own deed, and not chance, should undo them.
The tares they had laughingly sown were ripe to the reaping.

The trust they had leagued to disown was removed from their keeping.
The eaters of other men's bread, the exempted from hardship,
The excusers of impotence fled, abdicating their wardship,
For the hate they had taught through the State brought the State no defender,
And it passed from the roll of the Nations in headlong surrender!

The Covenant

We thought we ranked above the chance of ill.
    Others might fall, not we, for we were wise—
Merchants in freedom. So, of our free-will
    We let our servants drug our strength with lies.
The pleasure and the poison had its way
    On us as on the meanest, till we learned
That he who lies will steal, who steals will slay.
    Neither God's judgment nor man's heart was turned.

Yet there remains His Mercy—to be sought
Through wrath and peril till we cleanse the wrong

By that last right which our forefathers claimed
When their Law failed them and its stewards were bought.
This is our cause. God help us, and make strong
Our will to meet Him later, unashamed!

The Craftsman

Once, after long-drawn revel at The Mermaid.
He to the overbearing Boanerges
Jonson, uttered (if half of it were liquor,
        Blessed be the vintage!)

Saying how, at an alehouse under Cotswold,
He had made sure of his very Cleopatra,
Drunk with enormous, salvation-contemning
        Love for a tinker.

How, while he hid from Sir Thomas's keepers,
Crouched in a ditch and drenched by the midnight
Dews, he had listened to gipsy Juliet
        Rail at the dawning.

How at Bankside, a boy drowning kittens
Winced at the business; whereupon his sister—
Lady Macbeth aged seven—thrust 'em under,
        Sombrely scornful.

How on a Sabbath, hushed and compassionate—
She being known since her birth to the townsfolk—
Stratford dredged and delivered from Avon
        Dripping Ophelia.

So, with a thin third, finger marrying
Drop to winedrop domed on the table,
Shakespeare opened his heart till the sunrise—
        Entered to hear him.

London wakened and he, imperturbable,
Passed from waking to hurry after shadows . . .
Busied upon shows of no earthly importance?
        Yes, but he knew it!

The Dead King

Who in the Realm to-day lays down dear life for the sake of a land more dear?
  And, unconcerned for his own estate, toils till the last grudged sands have run?
    Let him approach. It is proven here
Our King asks nothing of any man more than Our King himself has done.

For to him above all was Life good, above all he commanded
    Her abundance full-handed.
The peculiar treasure of Kings was his for the taking:
All that men come to in dreams he inherited waking.

His marvel of world-gathered armies—one heart and all races;
His seas 'neath his keels when his war-castles foamed to their places;
The thundering foreshores that answered his heralded landing;
The huge lighted cities adoring, the assemblies upstanding;
The Councils of Kings called in haste to learn how he was minded—
The Kingdoms, the Powers, and the Glories he dealt with unblinded.

To him came all captains of men, all achievers of glory,
Hot from the press of their battles they told him their story.
They revealed him their lives in an hour and, saluting, departed,
Joyful to labour afresh: he had made them new-hearted.
And, since he weighed men from his youth, and no lie long deceived him,
He spoke and exacted the truth, and the basest believed him.

And God poured him an exquisite wine, that was daily renewed to him,
In the clear-welling love of his peoples that daily accrued to him.
Honour and service we gave him, rejoicingly fearless;
Faith absolute, trust beyond speech and a friendship as peerless.
And since he was Master and Servant in all that we asked him,
We leaned hard on his wisdom in all things, knowing not how we tasked him.

For on him each new day laid command, every tyrannous hour,
To confront, or confirm, or make smooth some dread issue of power;
To deliver true judgment aright at the instant, unaided,
In the strict, level, ultimate phrase that allowed or dissuaded;
To foresee, to allay, to avert from us perils unnumbered,
To stand guard on our gates when he guessed that the watchmen had slumbered;
To win time, to turn hate, to woo folly to service and, mightily schooling
His strength to the use of his Nations, to rule as not ruling.
These were the works of our King; Earth's peace was the proof of them.
God gave him great works to fulfil, and to us the behoof of them.

We accepted his toil as our right—none spared, none excused him.
When he was bowed by his burden his rest was refused him.
We troubled his age with our weakness—the blacker our shame to us!
Hearing his People had need of him, straightway he came to us.

As he received so he gave-nothing grudged, naught denying,
Not even the last gasp of his breath when he strove for us, dying.
For our sakes, without question, he put from him all that he cherished.
Simply as any that serve him he served and he perished.
All that Kings covet was his, and he flung it aside for us.
Simply as any that die in his service he died for us!

Who in the Realm to-day has choice of the easy road or the hard to tread?
    And, much concerned for his own estate, would sell his soul to remain in the sun?
        Let him depart nor look on Our dead.
Our King asks nothing of any man more than Our King himself has done.

A Death-Bed

"This is the State above the Law.
    The State exists for the State alone."
[This is a gland at the back of the jaw,
    And an answering lump by the collar-bone.]

Some die shouting in gas or fire;
    Some die silent, by shell and shot.
Some die desperate, caught on the wire;
    Some die suddenly. This will not.

"Regis suprema voluntas Lex"
    [It will follow the regular course of—throats.]
Some die pinned by the broken decks,
    Some die sobbing between the boats.

Some die eloquent, pressed to death
    By the sliding trench as their friends can hear.
Some die wholly in half a breath.
    Some—give trouble for half a year.

"There is neither Evil nor Good in life
    Except as the needs of the State ordain."
[Since it is rather too late for the knife,
    All we can do is to mask the pain.]

Some die saintly in faith and hope—
    One died thus in a prison-yard—
Some die broken by rape or the rope;
    Some die easily. This dies hard.

"I will dash to pieces who bar my way.
    Woe to the traitor! Woe to the weak!"

[Let him write what he wishes to say.
    It tires him out if he tries to speak.]

Some die quietly. Some abound
    In loud self-pity. Others spread
Bad morale through the cots around . . .
    This is a type that is better dead.

"The war was forced on me by my foes.
    All that I sought was the right to live."
[Don't be afraid of a triple dose;
    The pain will neutralize half we give.

Here are the needles. See that he dies
    While the effects of the drug endure. . . .
What is the question he asks with his eyes?—
    Yes, All-Highest, to God, be sure.]

The Declaration of London

*("On the re-assembling of Parliament after the Coronation, the Government have no intention of
allowing their followers to vote according to their convictions on the Declaration of London, but insist on
a strictly party vote."— Daily Papers.)*

We were all one heart and one race
    When the Abbey trumpets blew.
For a moment's breathing-space
    We had forgotten you.
Now you return to your honoured place
    Panting to shame us anew.

We have walked with the Ages dead—
    With our Past alive and ablaze.
And you bid us pawn our honour for bread,
    This day of all the days!
And you cannot wait till our guests are sped,
    Or last week's wreath decays?

The light is still in our eyes
    Of Faith and Gentlehood,
Of Service and Sacrifice;
    And it does not match our mood,
To turn so soon to your treacheries
    That starve our land of her food.

Our ears still carry the sound

Of our once-Imperial seas,
Exultant after our King was crowned,
    Beneath the sun and the breeze.
It is too early to have them bound
    Or sold at your decrees.

Wait till the memory goes,
    Wait till the visions fade,
We may betray in time, God knows,
    But we would not have it said,
When you make report to our scornful foes,
    That we kissed as we betrayed!

Dedication

To the Seven Watchmen

Seven Watchmen sitting in a tower,
    Watching what had come upon mankind,
Showed the Man the Glory and the Power,
    And bade him shape the Kingdom to his mind,
'All things on Earth your will shall win you.'
    ('Twas so their counsel ran)
'But the Kingdom—the Kingdom is within you,'
    Said the Man's own mind to the man.
        For time, and some time—
As it was in the bitter years before,
    So it shall be in the over-sweetened hour—
That a man's mind is wont to tell him more
    Than Seven Watchmen sitting in a tower.

En-Dor

"Behold there is a woman that hath a familiar spirit at En-dor."
— I Samuel, xxviii. 7.

The road to En-dor is easy to tread
    For Mother or yearning Wife.
There, it is sure, we shall meet our Dead
    As they were even in life.
Earth has not dreamed of the blessing in store
For desolate hearts on the road to En-dor.

Whispers shall comfort us out of the dark—

Hands—ah God!—that we knew!
Visions and voices—look and hark!—
    Shall prove that the tale is true,
And that those who have passed to the further shore
May be hailed—at a price—on the road to En-dor.

But they are so deep in their new eclipse
    Nothing they say can reach,
Unless it be uttered by alien lips
    And framed in a stranger's speech.
The son must send word to the mother that bore,
Through an hireling's mouth. 'Tis the rule of En-dor.

And not for nothing these gifts are shown
    By such as delight our dead.
They must twitch and stiffen and slaver and groan
    Ere the eyes are set in the head,
And the voice from the belly begins. Therefore,
We pay them a wage where they ply at En-dor.

Even so, we have need off faith
    And patience to follow the clue.
Often, at first, what the dear one saith
    Is babble, or jest, or untrue.
(Lying spirits perplex us sore
Till our loves—and their lives—are well-known at En-dory . . . .

Oh the road to En-dor is the oldest road
    And the craziest road of all!
Straight it runs to the Witch's abode,
    As it did in the days of Saul,
And nothing has changed of the sorrow in store
For such as go down on the road to En-dor!

Epitaphs of the War

"EQUALITY OF SACRIFICE"

A. "I was a Have."
B. "I was a 'have-not.'"
[Together]. "What hast thou given which I gave not?"

A SERVANT
We were together since the War began.
He was my servant—and the better man.

A SON

My son was killed while laughing at some jest. I would I knew
What it was, and it might serve me in a time when jests are few.

AN ONLY SON

I have slain none except my Mother.
She (Blessing her slayer) died of grief for me.

EX-CLERK

Pity not! The Army gave
Freedom to a timid slave:
In which Freedom did he find
Strength of body, will, and mind:
By which strength he came to prove
Mirth, Companionship, and Love:
For which Love to Death he went:
In which Death he lies content.

THE WONDER

Body and Spirit I surrendered whole
To harsh Instructors—and received a soul . . .
If mortal man could change me through and through
From all I was—what may The God not do?

HINDU SEPOY IN FRANCE

This man in his own country prayed we know not to what Powers.
We pray Them to reward him for his bravery in ours.

THE COWARD

I could not look on Death, which being known,
Men led me to him, blindfold and alone.

SHOCK

My name, my speech, my self I had forgot.
My wife and children came—I knew them not.
I died. My Mother followed. At her call
And on her bosom I remembered all.

A GRAVE NEAR CAIRO

Gods of the Nile, should this stout fellow here
Get out—get out! He knows not shame nor fear.

PELICANS IN THE WILDERNESS

[A Grave Near Halfa]
The blown sand heaps on me, that none may learn
   Where I am laid for whom my children grieve. . . .
O wings that beat at dawning, ye return
   Out of the desert to your young at eve!

THE FAVOUR
Death favoured me from the first, well knowing I could not endure
    To wait on him day by day. He quitted my betters and came
Whistling over the fields, and, when he had made all sure,
    "Thy line is at end," he said, "but at least I have saved its name."

THE BEGINNER
On the first hour of my first day
    In the front trench I fell.
(Children in boxes at a play
    Stand up to watch it well.)

R.A.F. (AGED EIGHTEEN)
Laughing through clouds, his milk-teeth still unshed,
Cities and men he smote from overhead.
His deaths delivered, he returned to play
Childlike, with childish things now put away.

THE REFINED MAN
I was of delicate mind. I stepped aside for my needs,
    Disdaining the common office. I was seen from afar and killed. . . .
How is this matter for mirth? Let each man be judged by his deeds.
    I have paid my price to live with myself on the terms that I willed.

NATIVE WATER-CARRIER (M.E.F.)
Prometheus brought down fire to men.
    This brought up water.
The Gods are jealous—now, as then,
    Giving no quarter.

BOMBED IN LONDON
On land and sea I strove with anxious care
To escape conscription. It was in the air!

THE SLEEPY SENTINEL
Faithless the watch that I kept: now I have none to keep.
I was slain because I slept: now I am slain I sleep.
Let no man reproach me again; whatever watch is unkept—
I sleep because I am slain. They slew me because I slept.

BATTERIES OUT OF AMMUNITION
If any mourn us in the workshop, say
We died because the shift kept holiday.

COMMON FORM
If any question why we died,
Tell them, because our fathers lied.

A DEAD STATESMAN

I could not dig: I dared not rob:
Therefore I lied to please the mob.
Now all my lies are proved untrue
And I must face the men I slew.
What tale shall serve me here among
Mine angry and defrauded young?

THE REBEL

If I had clamoured at Thy Gate
    For gift of Life on Earth,
And, thrusting through the souls that wait,
    Flung headlong into birth—
Even then, even then, for gin and snare
    About my pathway spread,
Lord, I had mocked Thy thoughtful care
    Before I joined the Dead!
But now? . . . I was beneath Thy Hand
    Ere yet the Planets came.
And now—though Planets pass, I stand
    The witness to Thy shame.

THE OBEDIENT

Daily, though no ears attended,
    Did my prayers arise.
Daily, though no fire descended
    Did I sacrifice.
Though my darkness did not lift,
    Though I faced no lighter odds,
Though the Gods bestowed no gift,
                None the less,
None the less, I served the Gods!

A DRIFTER OFF TARENTUM

He from the wind-bitten north with ship and companions descended.
    Searching for eggs of death spawned by invisible hulls.
Many he found and drew forth. Of a sudden the fishery ended
    In flame and a clamorous breath not new to the eye-pecking gulls.

DESTROYERS IN COLLISION

For Fog and Fate no charm is found
    To lighten or amend.
I, hurrying to my bride, was drowned—
    Cut down by my best friend.

CONVOY ESCORT

I was a shepherd to fools

Causelessly bold or afraid.
They would not abide by my rules.
    Yet they escaped. For I stayed.

UNKNOWN FEMALE CORPSE
Headless, lacking foot and hand,
Horrible I come to land.
I beseech all women's sons
Know I was a mother once.

RAPED AND REVENGED
One used and butchered me: another spied
Me broken—for which thing an hundred died.
So it was learned among the heathen hosts
How much a freeborn woman's favour costs.

SALONIKAN GRAVE
I have watched a thousand days
Push out and crawl into night
Slowly as tortoises.
Now I, too, follow these.
It is fever, and not the fight—
Time, not battle—that slays.

THE BRIDEGROOM
Call me not false, beloved,
    If, from thy scarce-known breast
So little time removed,
    In other arms I rest.

For this more ancient bride
    Whom coldly I embrace
Was constant at my side
    Before I saw thy face.

Our marriage, often set—
    By miracle delayed—
At last is consummate,
    And cannot be unmade.

Live, then, whom Life shall cure.
    Almost, of Memory,
And leave us to endure
    Its immortality.

V. A. D. (MEDITERRANEAN)
Ah, would swift ships had never been, for then we ne'er had found,
These harsh Ægean rocks between, this little virgin drowned,

Whom neither spouse nor child shall mourn, but men she nursed through pain
And—certain keels for whose return the heathen look in vain.

ACTORS
On a Memorial Tablet in Holy Trinity Church,
Stratford-on-Avon
We counterfeited once for your disport
    Men's joy and sorrow: but our day has passed.
We pray you pardon all where we fell short
    Seeing we were your servants to this last.

JOURNALISTS
On a Panel in the Hall of the Institute of Journalists
We have served our day.

The Female of the Species

When the Himalayan peasant meets the he-bear in his pride,
He shouts to scare the monster, who will often turn aside.
But the she-bear thus accosted rends the peasant tooth and nail.
For the female of the species is more deadly than the male.

When Nag the basking cobra hears the careless foot of man,
He will sometimes wriggle sideways and avoid it if he can.
But his mate makes no such motion where she camps beside the trail.
For the female of the species is more deadly than the male.

When the early Jesuit fathers preached to Hurons and Choctaws,
They prayed to be delivered from the vengeance of the squaws.
'Twas the women, not the warriors, turned those stark enthusiasts pale.
For the female of the species is more deadly than the male.

Man's timid heart is bursting with the things he must not say,
For the Woman that God gave him isn't his to give away;
But when hunter meets with husband, each confirms the other's tale—
The female of the species is more deadly than the male.

Man, a bear in most relations—worm and savage otherwise—
Man propounds negotiations, Man accepts the compromise.
Very rarely will he squarely push the logic of a fact
To its ultimate conclusion in unmitigated act.

Fear, or foolishness, impels him, ere he lay the wicked low,
To concede some form of trial even to his fiercest foe.
Mirth obscene diverts his anger—Doubt and Pity oft perplex
Him in dealing with an issue—to the scandal of The Sex!

But the Woman that God gave him, every fibre of her frame
Proves her launched for one sole issue, armed and engined for the same;
And to serve that single issue, lest the generations fail,
The female of the species must be deadlier than the male.

She who faces Death by torture for each life beneath her breast
May not deal in doubt or pity—must not swerve for fact or jest.
These be purely male diversions—not in these her honour dwells.
She the Other Law we live by, is that Law and nothing else.

She can bring no more to living than the powers that make her great
As the Mother of the Infant and the Mistress of the Mate.
And when Babe and Man are lacking and she strides unclaimed to claim
Her right as femme (and baron), her equipment is the same.

She is wedded to convictions—in default of grosser ties;
Her contentions are her children, Heaven help him who denies!—
He will meet no suave discussion, but the instant, white-hot, wild,
Wakened female of the species warring as for spouse and child.

Unprovoked and awful charges—even so the she-bear fights,
Speech that drips, corrodes, and poisons—even so the cobra bites,
Scientific vivisection of one nerve till it is raw
And the victim writhes in anguish—like the Jesuit with the squaw!

So it comes that Man, the coward, when he gathers to confer
With his fellow-braves in council, dare not leave a place for her
Where, at war with Life and Conscience, he uplifts his erring hands
To some God of Abstract justice—which no woman understands.

And Man knows it! Knows, moreover, that the Woman that God gave him
Must command but may not govern—shall enthral but not enslave him.
And She knows, because She warns him, and Her instincts never fail,
That the Female of Her Species is more deadly than the Male.

"For All We Have and Are"

For all we have and are,
For all our children's fate,
Stand up and take the war.
The Hun is at the gate!
Our world has passed away
In wantonness o'erthrown.
There is nothing left to-day
But steel and fire and stone!

Though all we knew depart,
The old Commandments stand—
"In courage keep your heart,
In strength lift up your hand."

Once more we hear the word
That sickened earth of old:—
"No law except the Sword
Unsheathed and uncontrolled."
Once more it knits mankind
Once more the nations go
To meet and break and bind
A crazed and driven foe.

Comfort, content, delight,
The ages' slow-bought gain,
They shrivelled in a night.
Only ourselves remain
To face the naked days
In silent fortitude,
Through perils and dismays
Renewed and re-renewed.
Though all we made depart,
The old Commandments stand:—
"In patience keep your heart,
In strength lift up your hand."

No easy hope or lies
Shall bring us to our goal,
But iron sacrifice
Of body, will, and soul.
There is but one task for all—
One life for each to give.
What stands if Freedom fall?
Who dies if England live?

France

Broke to every known mischance, lifted over all
By the light sane joy of life, the buckler of the Gaul;
Furious in luxury, merciless in toil,
Terrible with strength that draws from her tireless soil;
Strictest judge of her own worth, gentlest of man's mind,
First to follow Truth and last to leave old Truths behind—
France, beloved of every soul that loves its fellow-kind;

Ere our birth (rememberest thou?) side by side we lay
Fretting in the womb of Rome to begin our fray.
Ere men knew our tongues apart, our one task was known—
Each to mould the other's fate as he wrought his own.
To this end we stirred mankind till all Earth was ours,
Till our world-end strifes begat wayside Thrones and Powers—
Puppets that we made or broke to bar the other's path—
Necessary, outpost-folk, hirelings of our wrath.
To this end we stormed the seas, tack for tack, and burst
Through the doorways of new worlds, doubtful which was first,
Hand on hilt (rememberest thou?) ready for the blow—
Sure, whatever else we met, we should meet our foe.
Spurred or balked at every stride by the other's strength,
So we rode the ages down and every ocean's length!

Where did you refrain from us or we refrain from you?
Ask the wave that has not watched war between us two!
Others held us for a while, but with weaker charms,
These we quitted at the call for each other's arms.
Eager toward the known delight, equally we strove—
Each the other's mystery, terror, need, and love.
To each other's open court with our proofs we came.
Where could we find honour else, or men to test our claim?
From each other's throat we wrenched—valour's last reward—
That extorted word of praise gasped 'twixt lunge and guard.
In each other's cup we poured mingled blood and tears,
Brutal joys, unmeasured hopes, intolerable fears—
All that soiled or salted life for a thousand years.
Proved beyond the need of proof, matched in every clime,
O Companion, we have lived greatly through all time!

Yoked in knowledge and remorse, now we come to rest,
Laughing at old villainies that Time has turned to jest;
Pardoning old necessities no pardon can efface—
That undying sin we shared in Rouen market-place.
Now we watch the new years shape, wondering if they hold
Fiercer lightnings in their heart than we launched of old.
Now we hear new voices rise, question, boast or gird,
As we raged (rememberest thou?) when our crowds were stirred.
Now we count new keels afloat, and new hosts on land,
Massed like ours (rememberest thou?) when our strokes were planned.
We were schooled for dear life's sake, to know each other's blade.
What can Blood and Iron make more than we have made?
We have learned by keenest use to know each other's mind.
What shall Blood and Iron loose that we cannot bind?
We who swept each other's coast, sacked each other's home,
Since the sword of Brennus clashed on the scales at Rome
Listen, count and close again, wheeling girth to girth,

In the linked and steadfast guard set for peace on earth!

Broke to every known mischance, lifted over all
By the light sane joy of life, the buckler of the Gaul;
Furious in luxury, merciless in toil,
Terrible with strength renewed from a tireless soil;
Strictest judge of her own worth, gentlest of man's mind,
First to face the Truth and last to leave old Truths behind—
France, beloved of every soul that loves or serves its kind!

Gehazi

"Whence comest thou, Gehazi,
    So reverend to behold,
In scarlet and in ermines
    And chain of England's gold?"
"From following after Naaman
    To tell him all is well,
Whereby my zeal hath made me
    A Judge in Israel."

Well done, well done, Gehazi!
    Stretch forth thy ready hand,
Thou barely 'scaped from judgment,
    Take oath to judge the land
Unswayed by gift of money
    Or privy bribe, more base,
Of knowledge which is profit
    In any market-place.

Search out and probe, Gehazi,
    As thou of all canst try,
The truthful, well-weighed answer
    That tells the blacker lie—
The loud, uneasy virtue
    The anger feigned at will,
To overbear a witness
    And make the Court keep still.

Take order now, Gehazi,
    That no man talk aside
In secret with his judges
    The while his case is triect.
Lest he should show them—reason
    To keep a matter hid,
And subtly lead the questions

Away from what he did.

Thou mirror of uprightness,
   What ails thee at thy vows?
What means the risen whiteness
   Of the skin between thy brows?
The boils that shine and burrow,
   The sores that slough and bleed—
The leprosy of Naaman
   On thee and all thy seed?
     Stand up, stand up, Gehazi,
       Draw close thy robe and go,
     Gehazi, Judge in Israel,
       A leper white as snow!

Gethsemane

The Garden called Gethsemane
   In Picardy it was,
And there the people came to see
   The English soldiers pass,

We used to pass—we used to pass
   Or halt, as it might be,
And ship our masks in case of gas
   Beyond Gethsemane.

The Garden called Gethsemane,
   It held a pretty lass,
But all the time she talked to me
   I prayed my cup might pass.

The officer sat on the chair,
   The men lay on the grass,
And all the time we halted there
   I prayed my cup might pass.

It didn't pass—it didn't pass—
   It didn't pass from me.
I drank it when we met the gas
   Beyond Gethsemane.

The Holy War

"For here lay the excellent wisdom of him that built Mansoul, that the walls could never be broken down nor hurt by the most mighty adverse potentate unless the townsmen gave consent thereto."
— *BUNYAN'S Holy War.*

Tinker out of Bedford,
    A vagrant oft in quod,
A private under Fairfax,
    A minister of God—
Two hundred years and thirty
    Ere Armageddon came
His single hand portrayed it,
    And Bunyan was his name!

He mapped for those who follow,
    The world in which we are—
"This famous town of Mansoul"
    That takes the Holy War.
Her true and traitor people,
    The gates along her wall,
From Eye Gate unto Feel Gate,
    John Bunyan showed them all.

All enemy divisions,
    Recruits of every class,
And highly-screened positions
    For flame or poison-gas;
The craft that we call modern,
    The crimes that we call new,
John Bunyan had 'em typed and filed
    In Sixteen Eighty-two.

Likewise the Lords of Looseness
    That hamper faith and works,
The Perseverance-Doubters,
    And Present-Comfort shirks,
With brittle intellectuals
    Who crack beneath a strain—
John Bunyan met that helpful set
    In Charles the Second's reign.

Emmanuel's vanguard dying
    For right and not for rights,
My Lord Apollyon lying
    To the State-kept Stocholmites,
The Pope, the swithering Neutrals,
    The Kaiser and his Gott—
Their roles, their goals, their naked souls—
    He knew and drew the lot.

Now he hath left his quarters,
    In Bunhill Fields to lie,
The wisdom that he taught us
    Is proven prophecy—
One watchword through our Armies
    One answer from our Lands:—
"No dealings with Diabolus
    As long as Mansoul stands!"

A pedlar from a hovel,
    The lowest of the low,
The Father of the Novel,
    Salvation's first Defoe,
Eight blinded generations
    Ere Armageddon came,
He showed us how to meet it,
    And Bunyan was his name!

The Houses

(A Song of the Dominions)

'Twixt my house and thy house the pathway is broad,
In thy house or my house is half the world's hoard;
By my house and thy house hangs all the world's fate,
On thy house and my house lies half the world's hate.

For my house and thy house no help shall we find
Save thy house and my house—kin cleaving to kind;
If my house be taken, thine tumbleth anon.
If thy house be forfeit, mine followeth soon.

'Twixt my house and thy house what talk can there be
Of headship or lordship, or service or fee?
Since my house to thy house no greater can send
Than thy house to my house—friend comforting friend;
And thy house to my house no meaner can bring
Than my house to thy house—King counselling King.

The Hyænas

After the burial-parties leave

And the baffled kites have fled;
The wise hyænas come out at eve
　　To take account of our dead.

How he died and why he died
　　Troubles them not a whit.
They snout the bushes and stones aside
　　And dig till they come to it.

They are only resolute they shall eat
　　That they and their mates may thrive,
And they know that the dead are safer meat
　　Than the weakest thing alive.

(For a goat may butt, and a worm may sting,
　　And a child will sometimes stand;
But a poor dead soldier of the King
　　Can never lift a hand.)

They whoop and halloo and scatter the dirt
　　Until their tushes white
Take good hold in the army shirt,
　　And tug the corpse to light,

And the pitiful face is shewn again
　　For an instant ere they close;
But it is not discovered to living men—
　　Only to God and to those

Who, being soulless, are free from shame,
　　Whatever meat they may find.
Nor do they defile the dead man's name—
　　That is reserved for his kind.

Justice

Across a world where all men grieve
　　And grieving strive the more,
The great days range like tides and leave
　　Our dead on every shore.
Heavy the load we undergo,
　　And our own hands prepare,
If we have parley with the foe,
　　The load our sons must bear.

Before we loose the word

That bids new worlds to birth,
Needs must we loosen first the sword
   Of Justice upon earth;
Or else all else is vain
   Since life on earth began,
And the spent world sinks back again
   Hopeless of God and Man.

A People and their King
   Through ancient sin grown strong,
Because they feared no reckoning
   Would set no bound to wrong;
But now their hour is past,
   And we who bore it find
Evil Incarnate held at last
   To answer to mankind.

For agony and spoil
   Of nations beat to dust,
For poisoned air and tortured soil
   And cold, commanded lust,
And every secret woe
   The shuddering waters saw—
Willed and fulfilled by high and row—
   Let them relearn the Law.

That when the dooms are read,
   Not high nor low shall say:—
"My haughty or my humble head
   Has saved me in this day."
That, till the end of time,
   Their remnant shall recall
Their fathers' old, confederate crime
   Availed them not at all.

That neither schools nor priests,
   Nor Kings may build again
A people with the heart of beasts
   Made wise concerning men.
Whereby our dead shall sleep
   In honour, unbetrayed,
And we in faith and honour keep
   That peace for which they paid.

The Irish Guards

We're not so old in the Army List,
    But we're not so young at our trade,
For we had the honour at Fontenoy
    Of meeting the Guards' Brigade.
'Twas Lally, Dillon, Bulkeley, Clare,
    And Lee that led us then,
And after a hundred and seventy years
    We're fighting for France again!
        Old Days! The wild geese are flighting,
            Head to the storm as they faced it before!
        For where there are Irish there's bound to be fighting,
            And when there's no fighting, it's Ireland no more!

Ireland no more!

The fashion's all for khaki now,
    But once through France we went
Full-dressed in scarlet Army cloth,
    The English—left at Ghent.
They're fighting on our side to-day
    But, before they changed their clothes,
The half of Europe knew our fame,
    As all of Ireland knows!
        Old Days! The wild geese are flying,
            Head to the storm as they faced it before!
        For where there are Irish there's memory undying,
            And when we forget, it is Ireland no more!

Ireland no more!

From Barry Wood to Gouzeaucourt,
    From Boyne to Pilkem Ridge,
The ancient days come back no more
    Than water under the bridge.
But the bridge it stands and the water runs
    As red as yesterday,
And the Irish move to the sound of the guns
    Like salmon to the sea.
        Old Days! The wild geese are ranging,
            Head to the storm as they faced it before!
        For where there are Irish their hearts are unchanging,
            And when they are changed, it is Ireland no more!

Ireland no more!

We're not so old in the Army List,
    But we're not so new in the ring,
For we carried our packs with Marshal Saxe

When Louis was our King.
But Douglas Haig's our Marshal now
    And we're King George's men,
And after one hundred and seventy years
        We're fighting for France again!
        Ah, France! And did we stand by you,
            Then life was made splendid with gifts and rewards?
        Ah, France! And will we deny you
            In the hour of your agony, Mother of Swords?
        Old Days! The wild geese are flighting,
            Head to the storm as they faced it before!
        For where there are Irish there's loving and fighting,
            And when we stop either, it's Ireland no more!

Ireland no more!

Lord Roberts

He passed in the very battle-smoke
    Of the war that he had descried.
Three hundred mile of cannon spoke
    When the Master-Gunner died.

He passed to the very sound of the guns;
    But, before his eye grew dim,
He had seen the faces of the sons
    Whose sires had served with him.

He had touched their sword-hilts and greeted each
    With the old sure word of praise;
And there was virtue in touch and speech
    As it had been in old days.

So he dismissed them and took his rest,
    And the steadfast spirit went forth
Between the adoring East and West
    And the tireless guns of the North.

Clean, simple, valiant, well-beloved,
    Flawless in faith and fame,
Whom neither ease nor honours moved
    An hair's-breadth from his aim.

Never again the war-wise face,
    The weighed and urgent word
That pleaded in the market-place—

Pleaded and was not heard!

Yet from his life a new life springs
    Through all the hosts to come,
And Glory is the least of things
    That follow this man home.

Mary's Son

If you stop to find out what your wages will be
    And how they will clothe and feed you,
Willie, my son, don't you go on the Sea,
    For the Sea will never need you.

If you ask for the reason of every command,
    And argue with people about you,
Willie, my son, don't you go on the Land,
    For the Land will do better without you.

If you stop to consider the work you have done
    And to boast what your labour is worth, dear,
Angels may come for you, Willie, my son,
    But you'll never be wanted on Earth, dear!

Mesopotamia

They shall not return to us, the resolute, the young
    The eager and whole-hearted whom we gave:
But the men who left them thriftily to die in their own dung,
    Shall they come with years and honour to the grave?

They shall not return to us, the strong men coldly slain
    In sight of help denied from day to day:
But the men who edged their agonies and chid them in their pain,
    Are they too strong and wise to put away?

Our dead shall not return to us while Day and Night divide—
    Never while the bars of sunset hold.
But the idle-minded overlings who quibbled while they died,
    Shall they thrust for high employments as of old?

Shall we only threaten and be angry for an hour?
    When the storm is ended shall we find
How softly but how swiftly they have sidled back to power

By the favour and contrivance of their kind?

Even while they soothe us, while they promise large amends,
    Even while they make a show of fear,
Do they call upon their debtors, and take council with their friends,
    To confirm and re-establish each career?

Their lives cannot repay us—their death could not undo—
    The shame that they have laid upon our race.
But the slothfulness that wasted and the arrogance that slew,
    Shall we leave it unabated in its place?

My Boy Jack

"Have you news of my boy Jack?"
    Not this tide.
"When d'you think that he'll come back?"
    Not with this wind blowing, and this tide.

"Has any one else had word of him?"
    Not this tide.
For what is sunk will hardly swim,
    Not with this wind blowing, and this tide.

"Oh, dear, what comfort can I find?"
    None this tide,
    Nor any tide,
Except he did not shame his kind—
    Not even with that wind blowing, and that tide.

Then hold your head up all the more,
    This tide,
    And every tide;
Because he was the son you bore,
    And gave to that wind blowing and that tide!

A Nativity

The Babe was laid in the Manger
    Between the gentle kine—
All safe from cold and danger—
    "But it was not so with mine,
      (With mine! With mine!)
"Is it well with the child, is it well?"

The waiting mother prayed.
"For I know not how he fell,
    And I know not where he is laid."

A Star stood forth in Heaven;
    The Watchers ran to see
The Sign of the Promise given—
    "But there comes no sign to me
        (To me! To me!)
"My child died in the dark.
    Is it well with the child, is it well?
There was none to tend him or mark,
    And I know not how he fell."

The Cross was raised on high;
    The Mother grieved beside—
"But the Mother saw Him die
    And took Him when He died.
        (He died! He died!)
"Seemly and undefiled
    His burial-place was made—
Is it well, is it well with the child?
    For I know not where he is laid."

On the dawning of Easter Day
    Comes Mary Magdalene;
But the Stone was rolled away,
    And the Body was not within—
        (Within! Within!)
"Ah, who will answer my word?
    The broken mother prayed.
"They have taken away my Lord,
    And I know not where He is laid."

"The Star stands forth in Heaven.
    The watchers watch in vain
For Sign of the Promise given
    Of peace on Earth again—
        (Again! Again!)
"But I know for Whom he fell"—
    The steadfast mother smiled,
"Is it well with the child—is it well?
    It is well—it is well with the child!"

PRIMITIVE

I ate my fill of a whale that died
   And stranded after a month at sea. . . .
There is a pain in my inside.
    Why have the Gods afflicted me?
Ow! I am purged till I am a wraith!
   Wow! I am sick till I cannot see!
What is the sense of Religion and Faith?
   Look how the Gods have afflicted me!

PAGAN

How can the skin of rat or mouse hold
   Anything more than a harmless flea?. . .
The burning plague has taken my household.
   Why have my Gods afflicted me?
All my kith and kin are deceased,
   Though they were as good as good could be,
I will out and batter the family priest,
   Because my Gods have afflicted me!

MEDIÆVAL

My privy and well drain into each other
   After the custom of Christendie. . . .
Fevers and fluxes are wasting my mother.
   Why has the Lord afflicted me?
The Saints are helpless for all I offer—
   So are the clergy I used to fee.
Henceforward I keep my cash in my coffer,
   Because the Lord has afflicted me.

MATERIAL

I run eight hundred hens to the acre
   They die by dozens mysteriously.
I am more than doubtful concerning my Maker.
   Why has the Lord afflicted me?
What a return for all my endeavour
   Not to mention the L.S.D!
I am an atheist now and for ever,
   Because this God has afflicted me!

PROGRESSIVE

Money spent on an Army or Fleet
   Is homicidal lunacy. . . .
My son has been killed in the Mons retreat,
   Why is the Lord aficting me?
Why are murder, pillage and arson
   And rape allowed by the Deity?
I will write to the Times, deriding our parson
   Because my God has afflicted me.

CHORUS

We had a kettle: we let it leak:
   Our not repairing it made it worse.
We haven't had any tea for a week. . . .
   The bottom is out of the Universe!

CONCLUSION

This was none of the good Lord's pleasure,
   For the Spirit He breathed in Man is free;
But what comes after is measure for measure,
   And not a God that afflicteth thee.

As was the sowing so the reaping
   Is now and evermore shall be.
Thou art delivered to thine own keeping
   Only Thyself hath afflicted thee!

The Oldest Song

For before Eve was Lilith—Old Tale

"These were never your true love's eyes.
   Why do you feign that you love them?
You that broke from their constancies,
   And the wide calm brows above them!

This was never your true love's speech.
   Why do you thrill when you hear it?
You that have ridden out of its reach
   The width of the world or near it!

This was never your true love's hair;
    You that chafed when it bound you
Screened from knowledge or shame or care,
    In the night that it made around you!"

"All these things I know, I know.
    And that's why my heart is breaking!"
"Then what do you gain by pretending so?"
    "The joy of an old wound waking."

The Outlaws

Through learned and laborious years
    They set themselves to find
Fresh terrors and undreamed-of fears
    To heap upon mankind.

All that they drew from Heaven above
    Or digged from earth beneath,
They laid into their treasure-trove
    And arsenals of death:

While, for well-weighed advantage sake,
    Ruler and ruled alike
Built up the faith they meant to break
    When the fit hour should strike.

They traded with the careless earth,
    And good return it gave:
They plotted by their neighbour's hearth
    The means to make him slave.

When all was ready to their hand
    They loosed their hidden sword,
And utterly laid waste a land
    Their oath was pledged to guard

Coldly they went about to raise
    To life and make more dread
Abominations of old days,
    That men believed were dead.

They paid the price to reach their goal
    Across a world in flame;
But their own hate slew their own soul
    Before that victory came.

I do not look for holy saints to guide me on my way,
Or male and female devilkins to lead my feet astray.
If these are added, I rejoice—if not, I shall not mind,
So long as I have leave and choice to meet my fellow-kind.
    For as we come and as we go (and deadly-soon go we!)
    The people, Lord, Thy people, are good enough for me!

Thus I will honour pious men whose virtue shines so bright
(Though none are more amazed than I when I by chance do right),
And I will pity foolish men for woe their sins have bred
(Though ninety-nine per cent. of mine I brought on my own head).
    And, Amorite or Eremite, or General Averagee,
    The people, Lord, Thy people, are good enough for me!

And when they bore me overmuch, I will not shake mine ears,
Recalling many thousand such whom I have bored to tears.
And when they labour to impress, I will not doubt nor scoff;
Since I myself have done no less and—sometimes pulled it off.
    Yea, as we are and we are not, and we pretend to be,
    The people, Lord, Thy people, are good enough for me!

And when they work me random wrong, as oftentimes hath been,
I will not cherish hate too long (my hands are none too clean).
And when they do me random good I will not feign surprise.
No more than those whom I have cheered with wayside charities.
    But, as we give and as we take—whate'er our takings be—
    The people, Lord, Thy people, are good enough for me!

But when I meet with frantic folk who sinfully declare
There is no pardon for their sin, the same I will not spare
Till I have proved that Heaven and Hell which in our hearts we have
Show nothing irredeemable on either side the grave.
    For as we live and as we die—if utter Death there be—
    The people, Lord, Thy people, are good enough for me!

Deliver me from every pride—the Middle, High, and Low—
That bars me from a brother's side, whatever pride he show.
And purge me from all heresies of thought and speech and pen
That bid me judge him otherwise than I am judged.   Amen!
That I may sing of Crowd or King or road-borne company,
That I may labour in my day, vocation and degree,
To prove the same in deed and name, and hold unshakenly
(Where'er I go, whate'er I know, whoe'er my neighbour be)

This single faith in Life and Death and to Eternity:
"The people, Lord, Thy people, are good enough for me!"

The Pro-Consuls

The over-faithful sword returns the user
His heart's desire at price of his heart's blood.
The clamour of the arrogant accuser
Wastes that one hour we needed to make good.
This was foretold of old at our outgoing;
This we accepted who have squandered, knowing,
The strength and glory of our reputations,
At the day's need, as it were dross, to guard
The tender and new-dedicate foundations?
Against the sea we fear—not man's award.

They that dig foundations deep,
    Fit for realms to rise upon,
Little honour do they reap
    Of their generation,
Any more than mountains gain
Stature till we reach the plain.

With no veil before their face
    Such as shroud or sceptre lend—
Daily in the market-place,
    Of one height to foe and friend—
They must cheapen self to find
Ends uncheapened for mankind.

Through the night when hirelings rest
    Sleepless they arise, alone,
The unsleeping arch to test
    And the o'er-trusted corner-stone,
'Gainst the need, they know, that lies
Hid behind the centuries.

Not by lust of praise or show
    Not. by Peace herself betrayed—
Peace herself must they forego
    Till that peace be fitly made;
And in single strength uphold
Wearier hands and hearts acold.

On the stage their act bath framed
    For thy sports, O Liberty!

Doubted are they, and defamed
   By the tongues their act set free,
While they quicken, tend and raise
Power that must their power displace.

Lesser men feign greater goals,
   Failing whereof they may sit
Scholarly to judge the souls
   That go down into the pit,
And, despite its certain clay,
Heave a new world towards the day.

These at labour make no sign,
   More than planets, tides or years
Which discover God's design,
   Not our hopes and not our fears;
Nor in aught they gain or lose
Seek a triumph or excuse.

For, so the Ark be borne to Zion, who
Heeds how they perished or were paid that bore it?
For, so the Shrine abide, what shame—what pride—
If we, the priests, were bound or crowned before it?

The Question

Also titled "The Neutral" 1

Brethren, how shall it fare with me
   When the war is laid aside,
If it be proven that I am he
   For whom a world has died?

If it be proven that all my good,
   And the greater good I will make,
Were purchased me by a multitude
   Who suffered for my sake?

That I was delivered by mere mankind
   Vowed to one sacrifice,
And not, as I hold them, battle-blind,
   But dying with open eyes?

That they did not ask me to draw the sword
   When they stood to endure their lot—
That they only looked to me for a word,

And I answered I knew them not?

If it be found, when the battle clears,
    Their death has set me free,
Then how shall I live with myself through the years
    Which they have bought for me?

Brethren, how must it fare with me,
    Or how am I justified,
If it be proven that I am he
    For whom mankind has died—
If it be proven that I am he
    Who, being questioned, denied?

1. *Attitude of the United States of America during the first two years, seven months and four days of the Great War.*

A Recantation

(To Lyde of the Music Halls)

What boots it on the Gods to call?
    Since, answered or unheard,
We perish with the Gods and all
    Things made—except the Word.

Ere certain Fate had touched a heart
    By fifty years made cold,
I judged thee, Lyde, and thy art
    O'erblown and over-bold.

But he—but he, of whom bereft
    I suffer vacant days—
He on his shield not meanly left—
    He cherished all thy lays.

Witness the magic coffer stocked
    With convoluted runes
Wherein thy very voice was locked
    And linked to circling tunes.

Witness thy portrait, smoke-defiled,
    That decked his shelter-place.
Life seemed more present, wrote the chip
    Beneath thy well-known face.

And when the grudging days restored
    Him for a breath to home,
He, with fresh crowds of youth, adored
    Thee making mirth in Rome.

Therefore, I humble, join the hosts,
    Loyal and loud, who bow
To thee as Queen of Song—and ghosts,
    For I remember how

Never more rampant rose the Hall
    At thy audacious line
Than when the news came in from Gaul
    Thy son had—followed mine.

But thou didst hide it in thy breast
    And, capering, took the brunt
Of blaze and blare, and launched the jest
    That swept next week the front.

Singer to children! Ours possessed
    Sleep before noon—but thee,
Wakeful each midnight for the rest,
    No holocaust shall free!

Yet they who use the Word assigned,
    To hearten and make whole,
Not less than Gods have served mankind,
    Though vultures rend their soul.

The Rowers

When Germany proposed that England should help her in a naval demonstration to collect debts from Venezuela.

The banked oars fell an hundred strong,
    And backed and threshed and ground,
But bitter was the rowers' song
    As they brought the war-boat round.

They had no heart for the rally and roar
    That makes the whale-bath smoke—
When the great blades cleave and hold and leave
    As one on the racing stroke.

They sang:— And steer her by what star,

If we come unscathed from the Southern deep
    To be wrecked on a Baltic bar?

"Last night you swore our voyage was done,
    But seaward still we go.
And you tell us now of a secret vow
    You have made with an open foe!

"That we must lie off a lightless coast
    And haul and back and veer,
At the will of the breed that have wronged us most
    For a year and a year and a year!

"There was never a shame in Christendie
    They laid not to our door—
And you say we must take the winter sea
    And sail with them once more?

"Look South! The gale is scarce o'erpast
    That stripped and laid us down,
When we stood forth but they stood fast
    And prayed to see us drown.

"Our dead they mocked are scarcely cold,
    Our wounds are bleeding yet—
And you tell us now that our strength is sold
    To help them press for a debt!

"'Neath all the flags of all mankind
    That use upon the seas,
Was there no other fleet to find
    That you strike hands with these?

"Of evil times that men can choose
    On evil fate to fall,
What brooding judgment let you loose
    To pick the worst of all?

"In sight of peace—from the Narrow Seas
    O'er half the world to run—
With a cheated crew, to league anew
    With the Goth and the shameless Hun!"

Russia to the Pacifists

God rest you, peaceful gentlemen, let nothing you dismay,

But—leave your sports a little while—the dead are borne this way!
Armies dead and Cities dead, past all count or care.
God rest you, merry gentlemen, what portent see you there?
    Singing:— Break ground for a wearied host
        That have no ground to keep.
        Give them the rest that they covet most . . .
        And who shall next to sleep, good sirs,
        In such a trench to sleep?

God rest you, peaceful gentlemen, but give us leave to pass.
We go to dig a nation's grave as great as England was.
For this Kingdom and this Glory and this Power and this Pride
Three hundred years it flourished—in three hundred days it died.
    Singing:— Pour oil for a frozen throng,
        That lie about the ways.
        Give them the warmth they have lacked so long
        And what shall be next to blaze, good sirs,
        On such a pyre to blaze?

God restyou, thoughtful gentlemen, and send your sleep is light!
Remains of this dominion no shadow, sound, or sight,
Except the sound of weeping and the sight of burning fire,
And the shadow of a people that is trampled into mire.
    Singing:— Break bread for a starving folk
        That perish in the field.
        Give them their food as they take the yoke . . .
        And who shall be next to yield, good sirs,
        For such a bribe to yield?

God rest you, merry gentlemen, and keep you in your mirth!
Was ever Kingdom turned so soon to ashes, blood, and earth?
'Twixt the summer and the snow—seeding-time and frost—
Arms and victual, hope and counsel, name and country lost!
    Singing:— Let down by the foot and the head—
        Shovel and smooth it all!
        So do we bury a Nation dead . . .
        And who shall be next to fall, good sirs,
        With your good help to fall?

A Song at Cock-Crow

"Ille autem iterum negavit"

The first time that Peter deniéd his Lord
He shrank from the cudgel, the scourge and the cord,
But followed far off to see what they would do,

Till the cock crew—till the cock crew—
After Gethsemane, till the cock crew!

The first time that Peter deniéd his Lord
'Twas only a maid in the palace who heard,
As he sat by the fire and warmed himself through.
Then the cock crew! Then the cock crew!
("Thou also art one of them.") Then the cock crew!

The first time that Peter deniéd his Lord
He had neither the Throne, nor the Keys nor the Sword—
A poor silly fisherman, what could he do,
When the cock crew—when the cock crew—
But weep for his wickedness when the cock crew?

The next time that Peter deniéd his Lord
He was Fisher of Men, as foretold by the Word,
With the Crown on his brow and the Cross on his shoe,
When the cock crew—when the cock crew—
In Flanders and Picardy when the cock crew!
The next time that Peter deniéd his Lord
'Twas Mary the Mother in Heaven Who heard,
And She grieved for the maidens and wives that they slew
When the cock crew—when the cock crew—
Tirmonde and Aerschott when the cock crew!

The next time that Peter deniéd his Lord
The Babe in the Manger awakened and stirred,
And He stretched out His arms for the playmates He knew—
When the cock crew—when the cock crew—
But the waters had covered them when the cock crew!

The next time that Peter deniéd his Lord
'Twas Earth in her agony waited his word,
But he sat by the fire and naught would he do,
Though the cock crew—though the cock crew—
Over all Christendom, though the cock crew!

The last time that Peter deniéd his Lord,
The Father took from him the Keys and the Sword,
And the Mother and Babe brake his Kingdom in two,
When the cock crew—when the cock crew—
(Because of his wickedness) when the cock crew!

A Song in Storm

Be well assured that on our side
   The abiding oceans fight,
Though headlong wind and heaping tide
   Make us their sport to-night.
By force of weather not of war
   In jeopardy we steer:
Then welcome Fate's discourtesy
   Whereby it shall appear,
      How in all time of our distress,
      And our deliverance too,
      The game is more than the player of the game,
      And the ship is more than the crew!

Out of the mist into the mirk
   The glimmering combers roll.
Almost these mindless waters work
   As though they had a soul—
Almost as though they leagued to whelm
   Our flag beneath their green:
Then welcome Fate's discourtesy
   Whereby it shall be seen, etc.

Be well assured, though wave and wind
   Have mightier blows in store,
That we who keep the watch assigned
   Must stand to it the more;
And as our streaming bows rebuke
   Each billow's baulked career,
Sing, welcome Fate's discourtesy
   Whereby it is made clear, etc.

No matter though our decks be swept
   And mast and timber crack—
We can make good all loss except
   The loss of turning back.
So, 'twixt these Devils and our deep
   Let courteous trumpets sound,
To welcome Fate's discourtesy
   Whereby it will be found, etc.

Be well assured, though in our power
   Is nothing left to give
But chance and place to meet the hour,
   And leave to strive to live,
Till these dissolve our Order holds,
   Our Service binds us here.
Then welcome Fate's discourtesy
   Whereby it is made clear,

How in all time of our distress,
As in our triumph too,
The game is more than the player of the game,
And the ship is more than the crew!

The Song of the Lathes

Being the words of the tune hummed at her lathe by Mrs. L. Embsay, widow

The fans and the beltings they roar round me.
The power is shaking the floor round me
Till the lathes pick up their duty and the midnight-shift takes over.
      It is good for me to be here!

Guns in Flanders—Flanders guns!
(I had a man that worked 'em once!)
Shells for guns in Flanders, Flanders!
Shells for guns in Flanders, Flanders!
      Shells for guns in Flanders! Feed the guns!

The cranes and the carriers they boom over me,
The bays and the galleries they loom over me,
With their quarter-mile of pillars growing little in the distance—
      It is good for me to be here!

The Zeppelins and Gothas they raid over us.
Our lights give warning, and fade over us.
(Seven thousand women keeping quiet in the darkness!)
      Oh, it's good for me to be here!

The roofs and the buildings they grow round me,
Eating up the fields I used to know round me;
And the shed that I began in is a sub-inspector's office—
      So long have I been here!

I've seen six hundred mornings make our lamps grow dim,
Through the bit that isn't painted round our sky-light rim,
And the sunshine through the window slope according to the seasons,
      Twice since I've been here.

The trains on the sidings they call to us
With the hundred thousand blanks that they haul to us;
And we send 'em what we've finished, and they take it where it's wanted,
      For that is why we are here!

Man's hate passes as his love will pass.

God made woman what she always was.
Them that bear the burden they will never grant forgiveness
        So long as they are here!

Once I was a woman, but that's by with me.
All I loved and looked for, it must die with me;
But the Lord has left me over for a servant of the judgment,
        And I serve His judgments here!

Guns in Flanders-Flanders guns!
(I had a son that worked 'em once!)
Shells for guns in Flanders, Flanders!
Shells-for guns in Flanders, Flanders!
        Shells for guns in Flanders! Feed the guns!

The Sons of Martha

The sons of Mary seldom bother, for they have inherited that good part;
But the Sons of Martha favour their Mother of the careful soul and the troubled heart.
And because she lost her temper once, and because the was rude to the Lord her Guest,
Her Sons must wait upon Mary's Sons, world without end, reprieve, or rest.

It is their care in all the ages to take the buffet and cushion the shock.
It is their care that the gear engages; it is their care that the switches lock.
It is their care that the wheels run truly; it is their care to embark and entrain,
Tally, transport, and deliver duly the Sons of Mary by land and main.

They say to mountains, "Be ye removèd." They say to the lesser floods "Be dry."
Under their rods are the rocks reprovèd—they are not afraid of that which is high.
Then do the hill-tops shake to the summit—then is the bed of the deep laid bare,
That the Sons of Mary may overcome it, pleasantly sleeping and unaware.

They finger death at their gloves' end where they piece and repiece the living wires.
He rears against the gates they tend: they feed him hungry behind their fires.
Early at dawn, ere men see clear, they stumble into his terrible stall,
And hale him forth like a haltered steer, and goad and turn him till evenfall.

To these from birth is Belief forbidden; from these till death is Relief afar.
They are concerned with matters hidden—under the earthline their altars are:
The secret fountains to follow up, waters withdrawn to restore to the mouth,
And gather the floods as in a cup, and pour them again at a city's drouth.

They do not preach that their God will rouse them a little before the nuts work loose.
They do not teach that His Pity allows them to leave their job when they damn-well choose.
As in the thronged and the lighted ways, so in the dark and the desert they stand,
Wary and watchful all their days that their brethren's days may be long in the land.

Raise ye the stone or cleave the wood to make a path more fair or flat;
Lo, it is black already with blood some Son of Martha spilled for that!
Not as a ladder from earth to Heaven, not as a witness to any creed,
But simple service simply given to his own kind in their common need.

And the Sons of Mary smile and are blessèd—they know the angels are on their side.
They know in them is the Grace confessèd, and for them are the Mercies multiplied.
They sit at the Feet—they hear the Word—they see how truly the Promise runs.
They have cast their burden upon the Lord, and—the Lord He lays it on Martha's Sons!

The Spies' March

"The outbreak is in full swing and our death-rate would sicken Napoleon. . . . Dr. M— died last week, and C— on Monday, but some more medicines are coming . . . We don't seem to be able to check it at all . . . . Villages panicking badly . . . . In some places not a living soul . . . . But at any rate the experience gained may come in useful, so I am keeping my notes written up to date in case of accidents . . . Death is a queer chap to live with for steady company."
— Extract from a private letter from Manchuria.

There are no leaders to lead us to honour, and yet with out leaders we sally,
Each man reporting for duty alone, out of sight, out of reach, of his fellow.
There are no bugles to call the battalions, and yet without bugle we rally
From the ends of the earth to the ends of the earth, to follow the Standard of Yellow!
        Fall in! O fall in! O fall in!

Not where the squadrons mass,
    Not where the bayonets shine,
Not where the big shell shout as they pass
    Over the firing-line;
Not where the wounded are,
    Not' where the nations die,
Killed in the cleanly game of war—
    That is no place for a spy!
O Princes, Thrones and Powers, your work is less than ours—
    Here is no place for a spy!

Trained to another use,
    We march with colours furled,
Only concerned when Death breaks loose
    On a front of half a world.
Only for General Death
    The Yellow Flag may fly,
While we take post beneath—
    That is the place for a spy.
Where Plague has spread his pinions over Nations and Dominions—

Then will be work for a spy!

The dropping shots begin,
   The single funerals pass,
Our skirmishers run in,
   The corpses dot the grass!
The howling towns stampede,
   The tainted hamlets die.
Now it is war indeed—
   Now there is room for a spy!
O Peoples, Kings and Lands, we are waiting your commands—
What is the work for a spy?
      (Drums)— Fear is upon us, spy!

"Go where his pickets hide—
   Unmask the shape they take,
Whether a gnat from the waterside,
   Or a stinging fly in the brake,
Or filth of the crowded street,
   Or a sick rat limping by,
Or a smear of spittle dried in the heat—
   That is the work of a spy!
      (Drums)— Death is upon us, spy!

"What does he next prepare?
   Whence will he move to attack?—
By water, earth or air?—
   How can we head him back?
Shall we starve him out if we burn
   Or bury his food-supply?
Slip through his lines and learn—
   That is work for a spy!
      (Drums)— Get to your business, spy!

"Does he feint or strike in force?
   Will he charge or ambuscade?
What is it checks his course?
   Is he beaten or only delayed?
How long will the lull endure?
   Is he retreating? Why?
Crawl to his camp and make sure—
   That is the work for a spy!
      (Drums)— Fetch us our answer, spy!

"Ride with him girth to girth
   Wherever the Pale Horse wheels
Wait on his councils, ear to earth,
   And say what the dust reveals.

For the smoke of our torment rolls
    Where the burning thousands lie;
What do we care for men's bodies or souls?
    Bring us deliverance, spy!"

Things and the Man

In Memoriam, Joseph Chamberlain

"And Joseph dreamed a dream, and he told it his brethren and they hated him yet the more."— Genesis xxxvii. 5.

Oh ye who hold the written clue
    To all save all unwritten things,
And, half a league behind, pursue
    The accomplished Fact with flouts and flings,
    Look! To your knee your baby brings
        The oldest tale since Earth began—
    The answer to your worryings:
        "Once on a time there was a Man."

He, single-handed, met and slew
    Magicians, Armies, Ogres, Kings.
He lonely 'mid his doubting crew—
    "In all the loneliness of wings"—
    He fed the flame, he filled the springs,
        He locked the ranks, he launched the van
    Straight at the grinning Teeth of Things.
        "Once on a time there was a Man."

The peace of shocked Foundations flew
    Before his ribald questionings.
He broke the Oracles in two,
    And bared the paltry wires and strings.
    He headed desert wanderings;
        He led his soul, his cause, his clan
    A little from the ruck of Things.
        "Once on a time there was a Man."

Thrones, Powers, Dominions block the view
    With episodes and underlings—
The meek historian deems them true
    Nor heeds the song that Clio sings—
    The simple central truth that stings
        The mob to boo, the priest to ban;
    Things never yet created things—

"Once on a time there was a Mean."

A bolt is fallen from the blue.
   A wakened realm full circle swings
Where Dothan's dreamer dreams anew
   Of vast and farborne harvestings;
   And unto him an Empire clings
      That grips the purpose of his plan.
   My Lords, how think you of these things?
      Once—in our time—is there a Man?

Ulster

"Their webs shall not become garments, neither shall they cover themselves with their works: their works are works of iniquity and the act of violence is in their hands."
— Isaiah lix. 6.

The dark eleventh hour
Draws on and sees us sold
To every evil power
We fought against of old.
Rebellion, rapine, hate,
Oppression, wrong and greed
Are loosed to rule our fate,
By England's act and deed.

The Faith in which we stand,
The laws we made and guard,
Our honour, lives, and land
Are given for reward
To Murder done by night,
To Treason taught by day,
To folly, sloth, and spite,
And we are thrust away.

The blood our fathers spilt,
Our love, our toils, our pains,
Are counted us for guilt,
And only bind our chains.
Before an Empire's eyes
The traitor claims his price.
What need of further lies?
We are the sacrifice.

We asked no more than leave
To reap where we had sown,

Through good and ill to cleave
To our own flag and throne.
Now England's shot and steel
Beneath that flag must show
How loyal hearts should kneel
To England's oldest foe.

We know the war prepared
On every peaceful home,
We know the hells declared
For such as serve not Rome—
The terror, threats, and dread
In market, hearth, and field—
We know, when all is said.
We perish if we yield.

Believe, we dare not boast,
Believe, we do not fear
We stand to pay the cost
In all that men hold dear.
What answer from the North?
One Law, one Land, one Throne
If England drive us forth
We shall not fall alone!

The Verdicts

Not in the thick of the fight,
    Not in the press of the odds,
Do the heroes come to their height,
    Or we know the demi-gods.

That stands over till peace.
    We can only perceive
Men returned from the seas,
    Very grateful for leave.

They grant us sudden days
    Snatched from their business of war;
But we are too close to appraise
    What manner of men they are.

And, whether their names go down
    With age-kept victories,
Or whether they battle and drown
    Unreckoned, is hid from our eyes.

They are too near to be great,
   But our children shall understand
When and how our fate
   Was changed, and by whose hand.

Our children shall measure their worth.
   We are content to be blind . . .
But we know that we walk on a new-born earth
   With the saviours of mankind.

The Veterans

Written for the gathering of survivors of the Indian Mutiny, Albert Hall, 1907

To-day, across our fathers' graves,
   The astonished years reveal
The remnant of that desperate host
   Which cleansed our East with steel.

Hail and farewell! We greet you here,
   With tears that none will scorn—
O Keepers of the House of old,
   Or ever we were born!

One service more we dare to ask—
   Pray for us, heroes, pray,
That when Fate lays on us our task
   We do not shame the Day!

The Virginity

Try as he will, no man breaks wholly loose
   From his first love, no matter who she be.
Oh, was there ever sailor free to choose,
   That didn't settle somewhere near the sea?

Myself, it don't excite me nor amuse
   To watch a pack o' shipping on the sea,
But I can understand my neighbour's views
   From certain things which have occurred to me.

Men must keep touch with things they used to use
   To earn their living, even when they are free;

And so come back upon the least excuse—
    Same as the sailor settled near the sea.

He knows he's never going on no cruise
    He knows he's done and finished with the sea
And yet he likes to feel she's there to use—
    If he should ask her—as she used to be.

Even though she cost him all he had to lose,
    Even though she made him sick to hear or see,
Still, what she left of him will mostly choose
    Her skirts to sit by. How comes such to be?

Parsons in pulpits, tax payers in pews,
    Kings on your thrones, you know as well as me,
We've only one virginity to lose,
    And where we lost it there our hearts will be!

Zion

The Doorkeepers of Zion,
    They do not always stand
In helmet and whole armour,
    With halberds in their hand;
But, being sure of Zion,
    And all her mysteries,
They rest awhile in Zion,
Sit down and smile in Zion;
Ay, even jest in Zion;
    In Zion, at their ease.

The Gatekeepers of Baal,
    They dare not sit or lean,
But fume and fret and posture
    And foam and curse between;
For being bound to Baal,
    Whose sacrifice is vain,
Their rest is scant with Baal,
They glare and pant for Baal,
They mouth and rant for Baal,
    For Baal in their pain!

But we will go to Zion,
    By choice and not through dread,
With these our present comrades
    And those our present dead;

And, being free of Zion
   In both her fellowships,
Sit down and sup in Zion—
Stand up and drink in Zion
Whatever cup in Zion
   Is offered to our lips!

Born in Bombay on 30th December 1865, Joseph Rudyard Kipling wrote short stories, poems and novels, a body of work whose reputation is in constant flux as his presentations and interpretations of empire are viewed within the changing context of empirical absolution in the twentieth century. Having spent the first five years of his life in India he felt a natural affinity for the country, though his upbringing had a distinctly colonial taste flavour. He was born in the Bombay Presidency of British India to Lockwood Kipling, an English art teacher and illustrator who took a position as professor of architectural sculpture in the Jeejeebhoy School of Art and Alice MacDonald, spoken of by the a Viceroy of India that "dullness and Mrs Kipling cannot exist in the same room". Though their presence in India was principally artistic and educational, rather than political, the company they kept and the establishments in which they kept it indicate an existence very much benefitting from the British Empire. Lockwood would later go on to assume a position as curator of the Lahore Museum, while working on various illustrations for Rudyard's writing, and various decorations for the Victoria and Albert museum in London. Much of his work, then, was coloured by the empire, whether in service to or benefitting from, and it was into this distinctly British experience of India that Rudyard was born.

Lockwood and Alice had met and fallen in love at Rudyard Lake in Rudyard, Staffordshire, and their affections for the area were so great they chose to refer to the lake in naming their first-born. Alice came from a family of four sisters, all of whose marriages were significant and well-arranged; moreover, Rudyard's most famous relative was Stanley Baldwin, Conservative Prime Minister on three occasions in the 1920s and 1930s. Kipling's sense of belonging in Bombay is found in 'To the City of Bombay' in the dedication to Seven Seas, a collection of poems published in 1900, which reads:—

> Mother of Cities to me,
> For I was born in her gate,
> Between the palms and the sea,
> Where the world-end steamers wait.

His parents considered themselves Anglo-Indians, and he would later assume this classification although he did not live there long. His first five years, which he describes as days of "strong light and darkness", ended when he and his three-year-old sister Alice were removed to Southsea, Plymouth, to board with Captain Pryse Agar Holloway and his wife Mrs Sarah Holloway, a couple who cared for the children of couples born in British India. They were there for six years and Kipling would later recall their time there with horror, describing incidents of cruelty and neglect and wondering whether it was these which speeded up his literary maturity, for "it made me give attention to the lies I soon found it necessary to tell: and this, I presume, is the foundation of literary effort".

Alice's time, by contrast, was relatively comfortable, Mrs Holloway hoping that she would marry her son, though this ambition would not come to fruition. They did have relatives in England, a maternal aunt Georgiana and her husband who lived in Fulham, London, in a house at which they spent a month each Christmas and which Kipling later described as "a paradise which I verily believe saved me". Their mother returned in 1877 and removed them from their custody with the Holloways. A year later he gained admission to the United Services College at Westward Ho! in Devon, a recently established school with the intention of readying boys for military service in the British Army. His time here was fraught physically, though emotionally it proved fruitful for he began several firm friendships with other boys at the school. Moreover, he found in it inspiration for the setting of his series of schoolboy stories, Stalky and Co, begun in 1899. Meanwhile, his sister Alice had returned to Southsea and was boarding with Florence Garrard, with whom he fell in love and on whom he modeled Maisie in his first novel, The Light That Failed, published in 1891. At sixteen he was found lacking in the academic perspicacity necessary to undertake a scholarship to Oxford University, his parents meanwhile lacking the wherewithal to finance him therein. As such his father sought a job for him in Lahore, Punjab, where he was now a museum curator. The position he found for his son was as assistant editor of the Civil and Military Gazette, a small local newspaper. Kipling left for India on 20th September 1882, arriving in Bombay on 18th October. "There were yet three or four days" rail to Lahore, where my people lived. After these, my English years fell away, nor ever, I think, came back in full strength".

The Gazette appeared six days of the week, year-round save for a short break at both Christmas and Easter. Its editor Stephen Wheeler was diligent but Kipling's writing was insatiable, and he came to consider the paper his "mistress and most true love". In the summer of 1883 Kipling visited Shimla, the colonial hill-station and summer capital of British India which was then called Simla. Chosen by the British owing to its resemblance of English climate and scenery (as far as was possible in India), it became the seat of the Viceroy of India for the six months on the plains which were too hot for the British temperament, and subsequently became a "centre of power as well as pleasure". Lockwood was asked to serve in the Church there, and his family became yearly visitors while Kipling himself would take his annual leave here from 1885-88. The value of this time is evident from the regularity with which Simla appears in his writing for the Gazette, which in his journals he describes the time as

> "....pure joy—every golden hour counted. It began in heat and discomfort, by rail and road. It ended in the cool evening, with a wood fire in one's bedroom, and next morn—thirty more of them ahead!—the early cup of tea, the Mother who brought it in, and the long talks of us all together again."

In 1886, his Departmental Ditties appeared, his first collection of verse, and brought with it a change of editor; Kay Robinson, Wheeler's replacement, was in favour of Kipling's creativity and granted him more freedom in that respect, even asking him to write short stories to appear in the newspaper. The vivacity of his writing was captured in a description of him by an ex-colleague at the Gazette, saying he "never knew such a fellow for ink—he simply revelled in it, filling up his pen viciously, and then throwing the contents all over the office, so that it was almost dangerous to approach him". While in Lahore, he had thirty-nine stories published in the Gazette between November 1886 and June 1887. Most of these are compiled in Plain Tales from the Hills, his first collection of prose, which was published in January 1888 in Calcutta, shortly after his 22nd birthday. In November 1887, he transferred from the Gazette to its much larger sister newspaper, The Pioneer, based in Allahabad. The pace of his writing remained, and in 1888 he published six collections of stories, Soldiers Three, The Story of the Gadsbys, In Black and White, Under the Deodars, The Phantom Rickshaw and Wee Willie Winkie, composed of some 41 stories. In addition, his position as The Pioneer's special correspondent in the Western region of Rajputna, he wrote many sketches which were later compiled in Letters of Marque and published in From Sea to Sea and Other Sketches, Letters of Travel.

A dispute in 1889 saw him discharged from The Pioneer, though by now he had been considering his future and sold the rights to his six volumes of stories for £200 and a small royalty, while the Plain Tales fetched £50, along with six months' salary from The Pioneer in lieu of notice. Using the money to undertake a pilgrimage to London, the literary centre of the British Empire, he left India on 9th March 1889, travelling via Rangoon, San Francisco, Hong Kong and Japan, then through the United States writing articles for The Pioneer which were also included in From Sea to Sea and Other Sketches, Letters of Travel. Arriving in England at Liverpool on October 1889, London and his literary début there beckoned.

His first task was to find a place to live, and he eventually settled on quarters in Villiers Street, Strand. The next two years saw several stories accepted by various magazine editors, the publication of the novel The Light That Failed, a nervous breakdown, the collaboration with Wolcott Balestier on the novel (uncharacterstically misspelt) The Naulhaka, and in 1891, following his doctors' advice, he embarked on a further sea voyage, travelling to South Africa, Australia, New Zealand and also returning to India. His plans to spend Christmas with his family were cut short on the news of Balestier's sudden death from typhoid fever, prompting an immediate return to London. Before he left, he had proposed to Balestier's sister Caroline Starr Balestier, with whom he had been having a hushed romance for just over a year. Back in London, Life's Handicap was published in 1891, a collection of short stories whose subject was the British in India, and British India. On 18th January 1892 aged 26 he married Caroline in the midst of an epidemic of influenza. Caroline was given away by Henry James, the famous and celebrated American author.

Honeymooning in Japan, they travelled via Vermont, America, to visit the Balestier estate, and upon arrival in Yokahama they found that their bank, The New Oriental Banking Corporation, had failed, though this loss did not deter them and they returned to Vermont, Caroline now pregnant with their first child. Renting a cottage on a farm for $10 per month, they lived a spartan existence and were "extraordinarily and self-centredly content". The named the residence Bliss Cottage, and it was here that the child was born, named Josephine, "in three foot of snow on the night of 29th December 1892. Her Mother's birthday being the 31st and mine the 30th we congratulated her on her sense of the fitness of things." While here, Kipling had his first ideas for the Jungle Books. Shortly after Josephine was born the couple moved in pursuit of more space and comfort, buying ten acres overlooking the Connecticut River from Caroline's brother. The house they built there was inspired by the Mughul architecture he encountered in Lahore, and was named Naulakha (this time correctly spelt) in honour of Wolcott. His literary output in four years here included the Jungle Books, a collection of short stories entitled The Day's Work, the novel Captain Courageous and a plethora of poetry, of which most notably the volume The Seven Seas and his Barrack-Room Ballads. Meanwhile, he enjoyed correspondence with the many children who wrote to him about the Jungle Books.

In between this writing, Kipling took regular visitors. Most notably Arthur Conan Doyle came, bringing golf clubs and staying for two days to give Kipling an extended golf lesson. Kipling enjoyed the game so much that he continued to play, even in winter with special red balls, though he found that the ice would lead to drives travelling two miles as they slid "down the long slope to the Connecticut River". Elsie, the couple's second daughter, was born in February 1896, and by this time it is thought that their marriage had lost its original spark of spontaneity and descended into routine, though they remained loyal to one another. By now, failed arbitration between the United States and England over a border dispute involving British Guiana incited Anglo-American tensions which, in May 1896, resulted in a confrontation between Kipling and Caroline's brother, resulting in his arrest and, in the hearing which followed, the destruction of Kipling's private life, leaving him exhausted and miserable and leading to their return to England.

They had settled Torquay, Devon, by September 1896, and he remained socially present and literarily productive. The success of his writing had brought him fame, and he had responded with a sense of duty to include in his writing elements of political persuasion, most notably in his two poems Recessional and The White Man's Burden, which caused controversy when they were published in 1897 and 1899 respectively. Many considered them anthemic to the empire, propaganda for the imperial mindset so prevalent in the Victoria era. Their first son, John, was born in August 1887. Another journey to South Africa began a tradition of wintering there, which continued until 1908. His reputation as Poet of the Empire saw him well-received by politicians in the Cape Colony, and he started the newspaper The Friend for Lord Roberts and the British troops in Bloemfontein. Back in England, they moved to Rottingdean, East Sussex, in 1897, and in 1902 he bought Bateman's, a house built in 1630, which was his home from until his death in 1936. Kim was published in 1902, after which he collected material for Just So Stories for Little Children, published a year later. Both he and Josephine developed pneumonia while visiting the United States, from which she later died.

This decade proved his most successful, being awarded the Nobel Prize for Literature in 1907, the prize citation reading "in consideration of the power of observation, originality of imagination, virility of ideas and remarkable talent for narration which characterise the creations of this world-famous author". He was the first English-language recipient. At the award ceremony in Switzerland, Carl David af Wirsén praised Kipling and the English literary tradition:

> The Swedish Academy, in awarding the Nobel Prize in Literature this year to Rudyard Kipling, desires to pay a tribute to the literature of England, so rich in manifold glories, and to the greatest genius in the realm of narrative that that country has produced in our times.

Following this achievement, Kipling published Rewards and Fairies, which contained If, voted Britain's favourite poem in a BBC opinion poll in 1995. He turned down several recommendations for knighthood and was considered for Poet Laureate, though this position was never offered to him.

The sense of perseverance, honour and stoicism in If prevailed in many of his opinions, including that on the First World War. Writing in The New Army in Training in 1915, he scorned those who refused conscription, considering

> ....what will be the position in years to come of the young man who has deliberately elected to outcaste himself from this all-embracing brotherhood? What of his family, and, above all, what of his descendants, when the books have been closed and the last balance struck of sacrifice and sorrow in every hamlet, village, parish, suburb, city, shire, district, province, and Dominion throughout the Empire?

This attitude saw him encourage his son, John, to go to war, and he was promptly killed at the Battle of Loos in September 1915, aged 18. Last seen during the battle stumbling blindly through the mud, screaming in agony after an exploding shell had ripped his face apart, Kipling would write—

"If any question why we died
Tell them, because our fathers lied"

—perhaps betraying the guilt he felt at encouraging his son to go to war and finding him a position in the Irish Guards through his friendship with commander-in-chief Lord Roberts, for whom he had established The Friend in Bloemfontein. His death inspired much of Kipling's successive writing, notably My Boy Jack and a two-volume history of the Irish Guards, considered one of the finest examples of regimental history. Ironically, though his writing and his political position had arguably cost John his life, after the war he became friends with a French soldier whose copy of Kim, kept in his breast pocket, had stopped a bullet and saved his life. For a while the book and the soldier's Croix de Guerre were with Kipling, presented as tokens of gratitude, and they remained in contact, though when Kipling learned of the soldier's child he insisted on returning both book and medal.

He kept writing until 1930, though at a considerably slower pace, and to less success. His death, already once incorrectly announced early by a magazine in a premature obituary (and to which he responded "I've just read that I am dead. Don't forget to delete me from your list of subscribers") came on 18th January 1936, at the age of 70, from a perforated duodenal ulcer. His coffin was carried by, among others, his cousin the Prime Minister Stanley Baldwin, and his marble casket covered by a Union flag. He was cremated at Golders Green Crematorium in Northwest London and his ashes are buried at Poets' Corner in Westminster Abbey, alongside the graves of both Charles Dickens and Thomas Hardy.

In conjunction with various earthly memorials which commemorate him, alongside his extensive writing, he has a crater on Mercury named after him. The question of memorial and monument is much-addressed in English Literature and, as various great authors and poets have agreed before Kipling's time, his memory lives on more vivaciously set in his words, far longer and better represented than it could set in stone.

Rudyard Kipling - A Concise Bibliography

Books
The City of Dreadful Night (1885, short story)
Plain Tales from the Hills (1888)
Soldiers Three (1888)
The Story of the Gadsbys (1888)
In Black and White (1888)
Under the Deodars (1888)
The Phantom 'Rickshaw and other Eerie Tales (1888)
Wee Willie Winkie and Other Child Stories (1888)
Life's Handicap (1891)
The Light that Failed (1891) (novel)
American Notes (1891) (non-fiction)
The Naulahka: A Story of West and East (1892) (with Wolcott Balestie)
Many Inventions (1893)
The Jungle Book (1894)
Mowgli's Brothers (short story)
Kaa's Hunting (short story)

Tiger! Tiger! (short story)
The White Seal (short story)
Rikki-Tikki-Tavi (short story)
Toomai of the Elephants (short story)
Her Majesty's Servants (originally titled Servants of the Queen) (short story)
The Second Jungle Book (1895)
How Fear Came (short story)
The Miracle of Purun Bhagat (short story)
Letting in the Jungle (short story)
The Undertakers (short story)
The King's Ankus (short story)
Quiquern (short story)
Red Dog" (short story)
The Spring Running (short story)
Captains Courageous (1896) (novel)
The Day's Work (1898)
A Fleet in Being (1898)
Stalky & Co. (1899)
From Sea to Sea and Other Sketches, Letters of Travel (1899) (non-fiction)
Kim (1901) (novel)
Just So Stories for Little Children (1902)
Traffics and Discoveries (1904) (24 collected short stories)
With the Night Mail (1905) A Story of 2000 A.D
Puck of Pook's Hill (1906)
The Brushwood Boy (1907)
Actions and Reactions (1909)
A Song of the English (1909) (with W. Heath Robinson illustrator)
Rewards and Fairies (1910)
A History of England (1911) (non-fiction with Charles Robert Leslie Fletcher)
Songs from Books (1912)
As Easy as A.B.C. (1912) (Science-fiction short story)
The Fringes of the Fleet (1915) (non-fiction)
Sea Warfare (1916) (non-fiction)
A Diversity of Creatures (1917)
Land and Sea Tales for Scouts and Guides (1923)
The Irish Guards in the Great War (1923) (non-fiction)
Debits and Credits (1926)
A Book of Words (1928) (non-fiction)
Thy Servant a Dog (1930)
Limits and Renewals (1932)
Tales of India: the Windermere Series (1935)
Something of Myself (1937) (autobiography)
The Elephant's Child (fiction)

Autobiographies and Speeches
A Book of Words (1928)
Something of Myself (1937)

Short Story Collections

Quartette (1885) – with his father, mother, and sister
Plain Tales from the Hills (1888)
Soldiers Three, The Story of the Gadsbys, In Black and White (1888)
The Phantom 'Rickshaw and other Eerie Tales (1888)
Under the Deodars (1888)
Wee Willie Winkie and Other Child Stories (1888)
Life's Handicap (1891)
Many Inventions (1893)
The Jungle Book (1894)
The Second Jungle Book (1895)
The Day's Work (1898)
Life's Handicap (1899)
Stalky & Co. (1899)
Just So Stories (1902)
Traffics and Discoveries (1904)
Puck of Pook's Hill (1906)
Actions and Reactions (1909)
Abaft the Funnel (1909)
Rewards and Fairies (1910)
The Eyes of Asia (1917)
A Diversity of Creatures (1917)
Land and Sea Tales for Scouts and Guides (1923)
Debits and Credits (1926)
Thy Servant a Dog (1930)
Limits and Renewals (1932)

Military Collections

A Fleet in Being (1898)
France at War (1915)
The New Army in Training (1915)
Sea Warfare (1916)
The War in the Mountains (1917)
The Graves of the Fallen (1919)
The Irish Guards in the Great War (1923)

Poetry Collections

Schoolboy Lyrics (1881)
Echoes (1884) – with his sister, Alice ('Trix')
Departmental Ditties (1886)
Barrack-Room Ballads (1890)
The Seven Seas (1896)
An Almanac of Twelve Sports (1898, with illustrations by William Nicholson)
The Five Nations (1903)

Collected Verse (1907)
Songs from Books (1912)
The Years Between (1919)
Rudyard Kipling's Verse: Definitive Edition (1940)
The Muse Among the Motors (poetry)

Travel Writing
From Sea to Sea – Letters of Travel: 1887–1889 (1899)
Letters of Travel: 1892–1913 (1920)
Souvenirs of France (1933)
Brazilian Sketches: 1927 (1940)

Collected Works
The Outward Bound Edition (1897–1937, 36 volumes)
The Edition de Luxe (1897–1937, 38 volumes)
The Bombay Edition (1913–38, 31 volumes)
The Sussex Edition (1937–39, 35 volumes)
The Burwash Edition (1941, 28 volumes)

Poems
Departmental Ditties and Other Verses (1886)
Barrack Room Ballads (1889, republished with additions at later times)
The Seven Seas and Further Barrack-Room Ballads (In various editions 1891–96)
The Five Nations (with some new and some reprinted and revised poems, 1903)
Twenty-two original 'Historical Poems' (1911)
Songs from Books (1912)
The Years Between (1919)

Posthumous Collections
Rudyard Kipling's Verse: Definitive edition
A Choice of Kipling's Verse, edited by T.S. Eliot

In addition Kipling wrote and published many hundreds of poems too numerous to include here.